JOURNEYS

Benchmark and Unit Tests

Grade 1

Printed in the U.S.A.

ISBN-13 : 978-0-54-736884-9
ISBN-10: 0-54-736884-4

11 0982 14 13 12

4500388580

Contents

Name ____________________ Date ______________

Reading

Read Together

Read the story. Then read each question with your teacher. Mark the space for the best answer to each question.

Pam Looks for a Friend

Pam is sad.

Pam can not play.

Pam does not have a friend here.

What can Pam do?

Pam can look for a friend.

A tan cat runs to Pam.

It is Tom.

Pam pets Tom.

A big dog runs to Pam.

It is Sam.

Pam pets Sam.

To the teacher: Read the directions and questions with children. Passages and answer choices should be read independently.

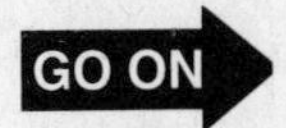

GO ON

Name ______________________ Date ____________

Pam looks at Tom and Sam.

Can Tom play?

Can Sam play?

Yes! They can play.

Tom and Sam play <u>tag</u> with Pam.

Pam has many friends here.

Pam is not sad.

Name ______________________ Date ____________

1 Which word tells how Pam feels at the start of the story?

- big
- mad
- sad

2 Read this sentence from the story.

Pam does not have a <u>friend</u> here.

What does the underlined word mean?

- pal
- like
- good

3 Read this sentence from the story.

Pam can <u>look</u> for a friend.

What does the underlined word mean?

- funny
- go find
- like to play

4 What happens right before a big dog runs to Pam?

- ⬭ Pam pets Tom.
- ⬭ Pam looks at Sam.
- ⬭ Tom and Sam play.

5 What happens right after Pam pets Sam?

- ⬭ Pam looks for a friend.
- ⬭ Pam looks at Tom and Sam.
- ⬭ Sam looks for Pam and Tom.

6 Read this sentence from the story.

Tom and Sam play <u>tag</u> with Pam.

Which picture shows what <u>tag</u> means in this sentence?

⬭ ⬭ ⬭

GO ON

Name ____________________ Date ____________

7 Which words tell how Pam feels at the end of the story?

- not sad
- not good
- a bit mad

8 Which of these words from the story comes first in ABC order?

- tan
- cat
- runs

GO ON

Name ______________________ Date ____________

Read Together

Read the selection. Then read each question with your teacher. Mark the space for the best answer to each question.

Many Jobs

The sun is up.

The man is up, too.

The man gets a mix.

He sets it in a tub.

The pigs run to it.

Yum! The pigs like the mix.

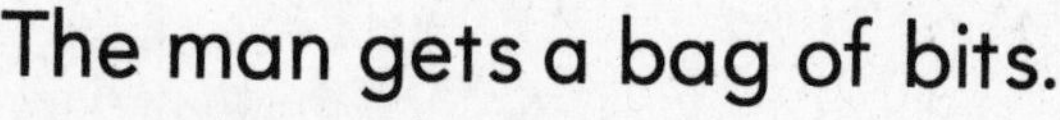

The man gets a bag of bits.

He tips the bag.

The hens run to get the bits.

Yum! The hens like the bits.

To the teacher: Read the directions and questions with children. Passages and answer choices should be read independently.

Name ______________________ Date ____________

The man gets a can.

He pops up the lid.

The cat runs to the man.

Yum! The cat likes it.

The man can not sit yet.

He has <u>many</u> jobs to do.

GO ON

Name ______________________ Date ____________

9 Read this sentence from the story.

<u>He</u> sets it in a tub.

What does the underlined word mean?

10 What happens right after the man sets a mix in a tub?

- The man gets up.
- The pigs run to it.
- The pigs play with the man.

GO ON

Name ______________________ Date ______________

11 What does the picture of the farmer feeding hens show you?

- ⬭ what is in the tub
- ⬭ what the pigs look like
- ⬭ what the hens look like

12 What happens right after the man gets a can?

- ⬭ The man sits.
- ⬭ He pops up the lid.
- ⬭ He gets a bag of bits.

13 Read this sentence from the story.

The cat runs to the man.

Which word in the sentence is an action verb?

- ⬭ The
- ⬭ cat
- ⬭ runs

Name ______________________ Date ______________

14 Read this sentence from the story.

He has <u>many</u> jobs to do.

What does the underlined word mean?

- ⬭ help
- ⬭ lots
- ⬭ sing

15 Which sentence tells the main idea of this story?

- ⬭ The man is up.
- ⬭ The pigs like the cat.
- ⬭ The man has many jobs.

STOP

Name ______________________ Date ______________

Reading: Phonics

Read Together

Read each sentence. Then mark the space for the word that best completes the sentence.

16 Look at the ______.

- ⬭ cat
- ⬭ cot
- ⬭ cut

17 Cat has a ______.

- ⬭ wag
- ⬭ web
- ⬭ wig

18 ______ is funny.

- ⬭ At
- ⬭ It
- ⬭ In

To the teacher: Read the directions with children. Items and answer choices should be read independently.

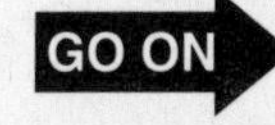

Name ______________________ Date ____________

19 The ________ plays, too.

- ⬭ fax
- ⬭ fix
- ⬭ fox

20 He ________ for the cat.

- ⬭ hop
- ⬭ hops
- ⬭ has

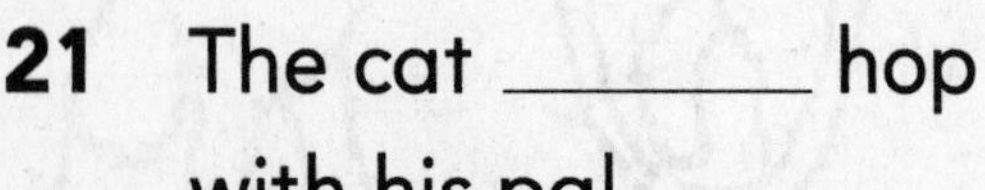

21 The cat ________ hop with his pal.

- ⬭ can
- ⬭ cot
- ⬭ cub

22 They have ________.

- ⬭ fan
- ⬭ fin
- ⬭ fun

GO ON

Name ______________________ Date ____________

23 The cat and fox are ________.

- ⬭ hat
- ⬭ hot
- ⬭ hut

24 What can the fox ________?

- ⬭ get
- ⬭ got
- ⬭ gut

25 The fox finds a ________.

- ⬭ fan
- ⬭ fin
- ⬭ fun

Name ______________________ Date ____________

Writing: Written Composition

Read Together

Draw a picture that shows something you did for the first time. Then write a label for your picture.

Read Together

REMEMBER, YOU SHOULD

- ❑ draw a picture that shows something you did for the first time
- ❑ write a short label that tells the main idea of your picture
- ❑ use the sounds in the words to help you write them

To the teacher: Read this page with children. Have them draw their picture on the following page. Direct them to write a label for the picture on the lines below it.

Name ______________________ Date ____________

DRAW YOUR PICTURE IN THIS BOX. WRITE YOUR LABEL BELOW YOUR PICTURE.

Name ____________________ Date ________

Reading

Read Together

Read the story. Then read each question with your teacher. Mark the space for the best answer to each question.

Friends

Miss Stock let the class <u>eat</u> a snack.

Jan got her box.
She will eat plums.

Kim did not pack a snack today.

Jan can help.
Jan will give Kim a plum.
Jan is a good friend.

To the teacher: Read the directions and questions with children. Passages and answer choices should be read independently.

Miss Stock let the class draw.

Kim got her pens.

She will draw pictures.

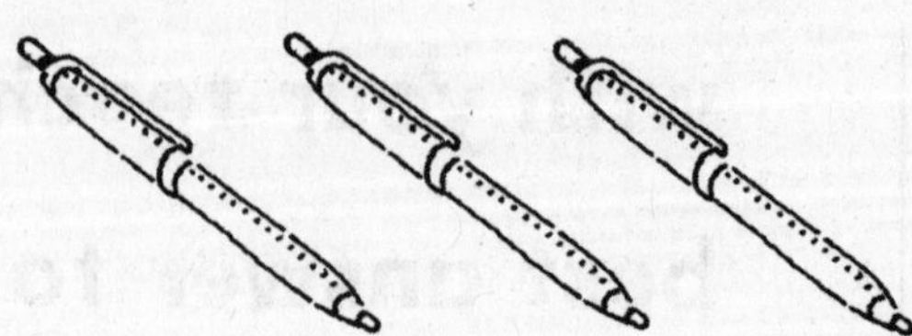

Jan did not pack pens today.

Kim can help.

Kim will give Jan some pens.

Now Kim is a good friend.

Kim and Jan are glad to be friends.

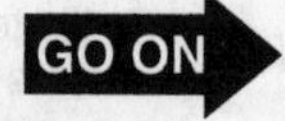

Name ______________________ Date ______

1 Where does the story take place?

2 Read this sentence from the story.

Miss Stock let the class eat a snack.

Which picture shows eat?

3 Why does Jan give Kim a plum?

- Kim does not have a snack.
- Jan does not like to eat plums.
- Miss Stock asks Jan to give a plum to Kim.

GO ON

4 Read this sentence from the story.

Miss Stock let the class <u>draw</u>.

Which picture shows <u>draw</u>?

5 Read this sentence from the story.

Kim got her pens.

Which word in the sentence is an action verb?

- ⬭ Kim
- ⬭ got
- ⬭ pens

GO ON

6 Use the chart to answer the question below.

Which sentence goes in the empty box?

- ⬭ Kim gets a box.
- ⬭ Kim has some plums.
- ⬭ Kim lets Jan have some pens.

7 Read this sentence from the story.

Now Kim is a good friend.

Which word in the sentence is a time word?

- ⬭ Now
- ⬭ Kim
- ⬭ good

8 Which sentence best tells about Kim?

- ⬭ She helps.
- ⬭ She has lots of plums.
- ⬭ She does not like to draw.

Name ______________________ Date ________

Read Together

Read the selection. Then read each question with your teacher. Mark the space for the best answer to each question.

How To Look After a Cat

My animal is a cat.

It is fun to have a pet.

You have lots of jobs!

Here are some jobs you must do.

Read the list.

A cat has to eat.

Put small bits in a pan.

To the teacher: Read the directions and questions with children. Passages and answer choices should be read independently.

GO ON

A cat has to sip.

Fill a pan for the cat.

A cat has to play.

Let it jump and run after you.

A cat has to nap.

Make a soft bed.

A cat would like a friend.

Give it a pat.

Do every job here.

You will have a glad cat!

9 What does the title tell you the selection will be about?

10 Read this sentence from the selection.

My <u>animal</u> is a cat.

Which picture shows another <u>animal</u>?

11 Read this sentence from the selection.

You have <u>lots</u> of jobs!

Which word means about the same as <u>lots</u>?

- like
- many
- one

GO ON

Name ______________________ Date ______

12 Read this sentence from the selection.

Put <u>small</u> bits in a pan.

Which word is the opposite of <u>small</u>?

- ⬭ big
- ⬭ fast
- ⬭ help

13 How does the first picture in the selection help you know more about how to look after a cat?

- ⬭ We see why the cat plays.
- ⬭ We see how the cat helps.
- ⬭ We see cat bits come in a bag.

14 Which job helps the cat take a nap?

- ⬭ Give it a pat.
- ⬭ Make a soft bed.
- ⬭ Fill a pan for the cat.

15 Why is it good to pat a cat?

- ⬭ A cat has to eat.
- ⬭ A cat has to nap.
- ⬭ A cat would like a friend.

Name ______________________ Date ______

Reading: Phonics

Read Together

Read the sentences. Then mark the space for the word that best completes each sentence.

16 Rick and Sam ________ what to put in the bag.

- ⬭ black
- ⬭ plan
- ⬭ plant

17 They get to take a ________.

- ⬭ clip
- ⬭ drip
- ⬭ trip

18 Dad puts the bags in the ________ of the van.

- ⬭ bats
- ⬭ back
- ⬭ ball

To the teacher: Read the directions with children. Items and answer choices should be read independently.

Name ______________________ Date ______

19 Some bags ________ not fit.

⬭ add
⬭ miss
⬭ will

20 Rick and Sam help Dad ________ up the bags.

⬭ lift
⬭ milk
⬭ pond

21 They help Dad ________ the bags on top of the van.

⬭ scrap
⬭ stack
⬭ swam

22 Dad gets a ________ to hold the bags to the top of the van.

⬭ strap
⬭ scamp
⬭ struck

GO ON

23 The bags will not ________ off the van now.

- ⬭ brag
- ⬭ crop
- ⬭ drop

24 Rick and Sam look at the ________.

- ⬭ clock
- ⬭ flat
- ⬭ slim

25 They ________ in the van to go.

- ⬭ camp
- ⬭ jump
- ⬭ dump

Name ______________________ Date ________

Writing: Written Composition

Read Together

Write a description of the animal you like best. Then draw a picture to go with your description.

Read Together

REMEMBER, YOU SHOULD

- ❑ write about how your animal looks, sounds, smells, and feels
- ❑ write a naming part and an action part in each sentence
- ❑ use the sounds in the words to help you write them
- ❑ begin each sentence with a capital letter

To the teacher: Read this page with children. Have them plan their description on a separate sheet. Direct them to the following lined page for writing and blank page for illustration.

Name ______________________ Date __________

Grade 1, Unit 2
UNIT TEST

Written Composition

BE SURE TO WRITE YOUR DESCRIPTION ON THESE LINES.

Name ______________________ Date ______

Grade 1, Unit 2
UNIT TEST

Written Composition

BE SURE TO DRAW YOUR PICTURE IN THIS BOX.

Name ________________ Date ________

Reading

Read Together

Read the story. Then read each question with your teacher. Mark the space for the best answer to each question.

Jill's New Cat

Jill felt glad. She would get a cat.

Dad and Jill went to a place that had lots of animals. The animals did not have a place to live. Jill and Dad went to see the cats.

A big white cat bumped Jill's leg. It had two blue eyes. Jill bent down and picked it up. The cat was soft.

To the teacher: Read the directions and questions with children. Passage and answer choices should be read independently.

Name ____________________ Date __________

"This is my cat," Jill said. "She will be a good friend for me."

"Do you see the little cat?" asked Dad. "A little cat will run and <u>play</u> with you."

"No, I picked the best cat," said Jill. "I will call her Puff."

Dad looked at the smile on Jill's face. He nodded. Puff would have a good place to live.

Name ______________________ Date ____________

1 Why does Jill feel glad at the start of the story?

- She will get a cat.
- She will run with Dad.
- She will play with animals.

2 Read this sentence from the story

It had two blue eyes.

Which word in the sentence is a color word?

- two
- blue
- eyes

3 Read this sentence from the story.

Jill bent <u>down</u> and picked it up.

What does the underlined word mean?

- not up
- in here
- too soft

GO ON

Name ______________________ Date ____________

4 What makes Jill pick up the cat?

- A cat bumps her leg.
- A little cat runs past her.
- She goes to a place that has animals.

5 Read this sentence from the story.

"A little cat will run and <u>play</u> with you."

What does the underlined word mean?

- grow
- rest
- have fun

6 Why does Jill name the cat <u>Puff</u>?

- The cat is white and soft.
- The cat puffs when it runs.
- The cat likes to play with puffs.

GO ON

Name ______________________ Date ____________

7 What happens right after Jill names the cat?

- ⬭ Dad nods.
- ⬭ The cat naps.
- ⬭ Jill picks up the cat.

8 Read this sentence from the story.

Dad looked at the <u>smile</u> on Jill's face.

What does <u>smile</u> mean in this sentence?

- ⬭ grape
- ⬭ grin
- ⬭ sick

GO ON

Name ______________________ Date ____________

Read Together

Read the selection. Then read each question with your teacher. Mark the space for the best answer to each question.

What Lives in a Pond?

A pond is a place filled with water. Plants and animals both live in a pond.

A fish is an animal. It has fins that flap. It has skin made of scales. The scales are flat. The fins and scales help the fish swim.

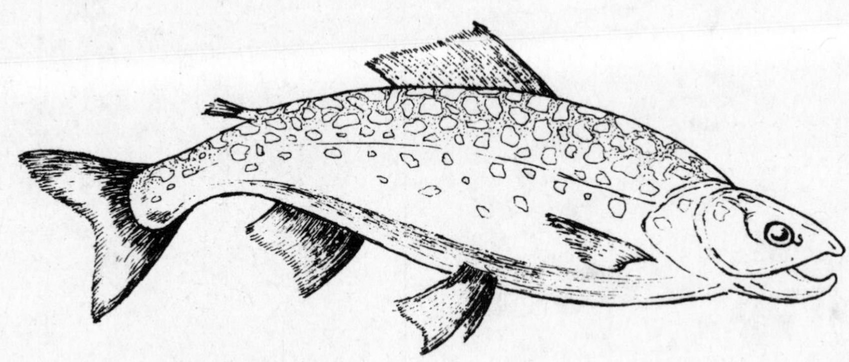

Read Together **To the teacher: Read the directions and questions with children. Passage and answer choices should be read independently.**

Name ________________________ Date ____________

A frog is an animal. It can live in water. It can live on the land, too. It has four legs. The two back legs are long. The back legs help the frog swim in water. They help the frog hop on land.

Grass is a plant. It grows in the mud of the pond. Fish and frogs swim into the grass. The grass helps them hide. Big animals can not see them. Then the big animals can not <u>eat</u> the fish and frogs.

Name ______________________ Date ____________

9 Read this sentence from the selection.

A pond is a place filled with <u>water</u>.

Which picture shows what the underlined word means?

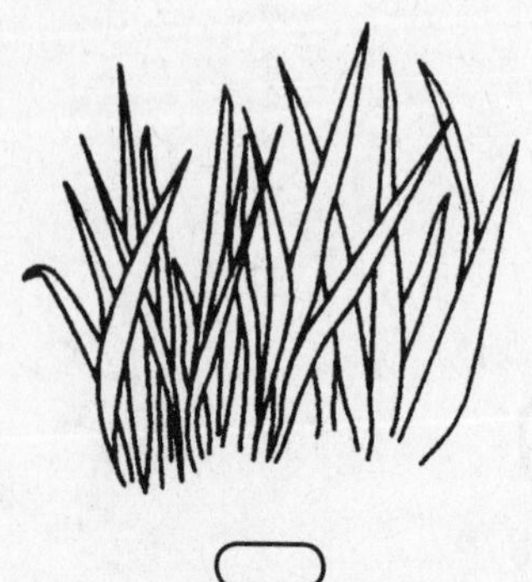

10 What helps fish swim?

- ⬭ legs and fins
- ⬭ fins and scales
- ⬭ scales and legs

11 Read this sentence from the selection.

The two back legs are long.

Which word in the sentence is a number word?

- ⬭ two
- ⬭ back
- ⬭ long

GO ON

Name ______________________ Date ____________

12 Which caption best tells about the picture?

- what fish look like
- how the frog hides
- when the frog hops

13 Read this sentence from the selection.

Then the big animals can not <u>eat</u> the fish and frogs.

Which picture shows what the underlined word means?

14 Which sentence tells the main idea of the selection?

- Fish and frogs swim into the grass.
- Plants and animals both live in a pond.
- The back legs help the frog swim in water.

15 Why did the author write the selection?

- to tell a funny tale
- to tell what is in a pond
- to get you to hike to a pond

Name ______________________ Date ____________

Reading: Phonics

Read Together

Read each sentence. Then mark the space for the word that best completes the sentence.

16 Jake's dog had to get a ______.

- back
- batch
- bath

17 The dog ______ like water.

- aren't
- didn't
- isn't

18 Jake had to ______ the dog.

- cast
- cash
- catch

To the teacher: Read the directions with children. Items and answer choices should be read independently.

Name ____________________ Date ____________

19 The dog went into the ______.

- ⬭ tab
- ⬭ top
- ⬭ tub

20 ______ all wet now!

- ⬭ He's
- ⬭ Let's
- ⬭ Aren't

21 The dog starts to ______.

- ⬭ fine
- ⬭ slime
- ⬭ whine

22 Watch out! The dog is going to ______.

- ⬭ shake
- ⬭ shine
- ⬭ shop

GO ON

Name ______________________ Date ____________

23 Did you see the water ______ on Jake?

- flash
- scratch
- splash

24 Look at the water ______ off Jake.

- clip
- drip
- dip

25 Jake and the dog are both ______!

- wit
- wet
- win

STOP

Name ______________________ Date ____________

Writing: Written Composition

Read Together

Write a letter to a friend telling her or him how to make your favorite snack.

Read Together

REMEMBER, YOU SHOULD

- ❑ write a letter that tells how to make your favorite snack
- ❑ make sure your letter has a date, a greeting, a body, a closing, and your name
- ❑ use order words, such as *first*, *next*, *then*, and *last*.
- ❑ use the sounds in the words to help you write them
- ❑ begin each sentence with a capital letter

To the teacher: Read this page with children. Have them plan their letter on a separate sheet of paper. Direct them to use the following lined pages for writing their letter.

Name ______________________ Date ____________

BE SURE TO WRITE YOUR LETTER ON THESE LINES.

Name ______________________ Date ____________

Name ______________________ Date ______

Reading

Read Together

Read the story. Then read each question with your teacher. Mark the space for the best answer to each question.

The Box

It is raining. Jess and Beth stay inside. They look for some things to do.

Jess and Beth find an old box. They walk around it. They want to know what is inside the box.

Jess and Beth carry the box to their mother. Mom opens it. The box holds old things.

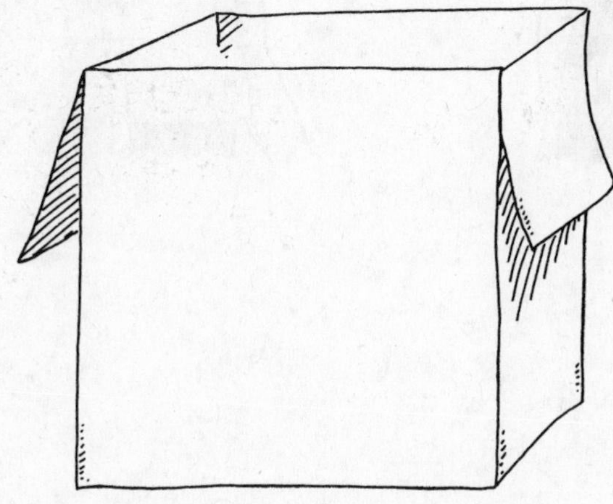

To the teacher: Read the directions and questions with children. Passages and answer choices should be read independently.

GO ON

"I played with these when I was little," Mom tells Jess and Beth.

Jess likes the boat. Beth likes the car.

Mom picks up a <u>small</u> box. It is gray. She lifts the top. The box <u>plays</u> a sweet tune.

GO ON

Name ______________________ Date ______

1 Why are Jess and Beth inside?

- ⬭ It is raining.
- ⬭ They are sick.
- ⬭ They must help Mom clean.

2 Read this sentence from the story.

Jess and Beth find an old box.

What does the word old mean in this sentence?

- ⬭ not new
- ⬭ too soft
- ⬭ very funny

3 What happens after Jess and Beth take the old box to Mom?

- ⬭ Mom opens the box.
- ⬭ Mom puts the box away.
- ⬭ Mom puts things in the box.

GO ON

4 Use the chart to answer the question below.

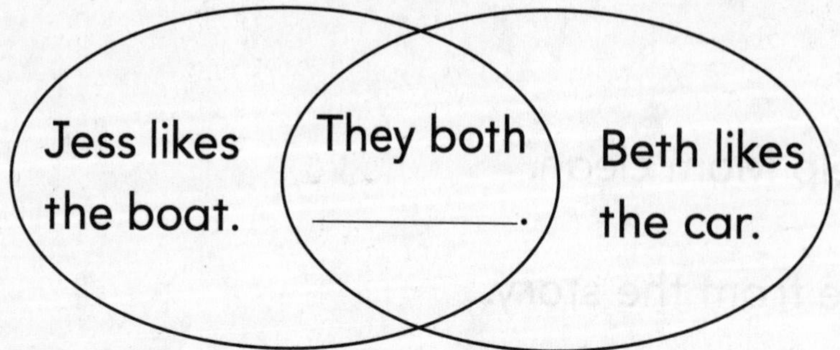

Which of these goes on the blank line to show how Jess and Beth are the same?

- like the rain
- open the box
- stay inside

5 Read this sentence from the story.

Jess and Beth carry the box to their mother.

What does the underlined word mean in this sentence?

- take
- sing
- like

GO ON

6 How are the boat and car the same?

- ⬭ They both have wheels.
- ⬭ Mom played with them both.
- ⬭ They both play a sweet tune.

7 Read this sentence from the story.

Mom picks up a <u>small</u> box.

Which word means about the same as small in this sentence?

- ⬭ brown
- ⬭ slim
- ⬭ little

8 Read this sentence from the story.

The box plays a sweet tune.

What does the word plays mean in this sentence?

- ⬭ has fun
- ⬭ makes a song
- ⬭ acts on a stage

GO ON

Name ______________________ Date ________

Read Together

Read the selection. Then read each question with your teacher. Mark the space for the best answer to each question.

A Note for You

A friend writes on paper. It is a note for you. She puts it in a mailbox. How do you get it?

To the teacher: Read the directions and questions with children. Passages and answer choices should be read independently.

First, someone gets the note. It goes in a bag. Then it goes to a mail place.

Next, someone looks at the Zip Code. The Zip Code tells where you live. Mail with the same Zip Code goes in one box.

A truck picks up the box. It drives to a mail place by you.

Someone reads your name and your street. She will <u>bring</u> the note to you.

9 Which sentence tells the main idea of "A Note for You"?

- Trucks bring the mail.
- Mail is put inside bags.
- You see how mail gets to you.

10 Read this sentence from the selection.

She puts it in a <u>mailbox</u>.

What does the word <u>mailbox</u> mean in this sentence?

- a box to put mail in
- a box on a truck
- a box that someone will mail

11 What is a Zip Code?

- the name of a street
- a code for where someone lives
- a fast truck that drives the mail

GO ON

12 Read this sentence from the selection.

A truck picks up the box.

Which word in this sentence is something to ride in?

- ⬭ truck
- ⬭ picks
- ⬭ up

13 Why does someone write a name on mail?

- ⬭ to tell who it is for
- ⬭ to tell who will drive the truck
- ⬭ to tell who will put it in a mail bag

14 Read this sentence from the selection.

She will <u>bring</u> the note to you.

What does the underlined word mean in this sentence?

- ⬭ lots of mail
- ⬭ take to a new place
- ⬭ someone who sends mail

15 Why did the author write "A Note for You"?

- ⬭ to tell a funny story
- ⬭ to tell facts about mail
- ⬭ to get you to send mail

Name ______________________ Date ________

Reading: Phonics

Read Together

Read each sentence. Then mark the space for the word that best completes the sentence.

16 Steve and Jay had a ________.

- ⬭ sleepover
- ⬭ into
- ⬭ sidewalk

17 The ________ came down.

- ⬭ rain
- ⬭ run
- ⬭ rent

18 "Let's play hide and ________," said Jay.

- ⬭ sack
- ⬭ seek
- ⬭ sick

To the teacher: Read the directions with children. Items and answer choices should be read independently.

GO ON

Name ______________________ Date ______

19 "I will ________ my eyes first," he said.

- ⬭ close
- ⬭ class
- ⬭ case

20 Steve ran up the steps and saw a ________ pile of quilts.

- ⬭ hug
- ⬭ huge
- ⬭ hung

21 Steve said, "Look at all ________ quilts!"

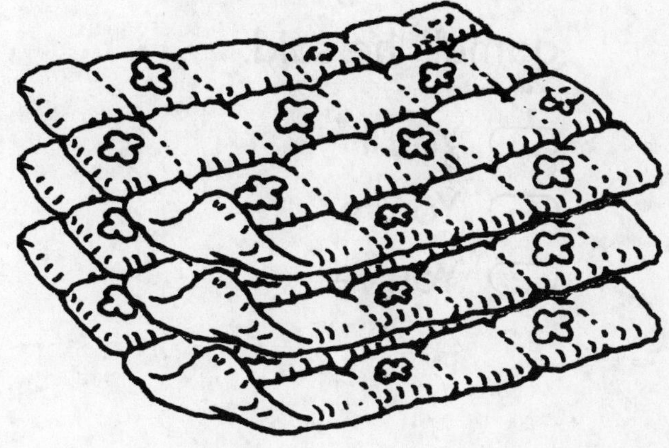

- ⬭ teach
- ⬭ then
- ⬭ these

22 "________ hide under them," he said.

- ⬭ I'll
- ⬭ Isn't
- ⬭ It's

GO ON

Name ______________________ Date ______

23 Steve pulled the quilts over his ______.

- ⬭ hay
- ⬭ hide
- ⬭ head

24 "I give up!" Jay ______. "Where are you?"

- ⬭ grand
- ⬭ groaned
- ⬭ grow

25 "______ good at this game!" he said.

- ⬭ You'll
- ⬭ You're
- ⬭ You've

STOP

Name ______________________ Date ________

Writing: Revising and Editing

Read Together

Read each question with your teacher. Decide which is the best answer. Then mark the space for the answer you have chosen.

1 Which word is spelled **wrong** in this sentence?

Lee sat under a tri.

- ⬭ sat
- ⬭ under
- ⬭ tri

2 Which word should have a capital letter in this sentence?

Soon it would be mother's Day.

- ⬭ it
- ⬭ would
- ⬭ mother's

3 Which word should have a capital letter in this sentence?

what gift would Lee get for Mom?

- ⬭ what
- ⬭ get
- ⬭ for

GO ON

Read Together **To the teacher: Read the directions and questions with children. Target sentences and answer choices should be read independently.**

4 Which is the correct way to write the date in this sentence?

Lee gave his mom a gift on May 10 2009.

- May 10, 2009
- May, 10 2009
- May 10 2009,

5 Which word is **wrong** in this sentence?

She opened it under lunch.

- opened
- under
- lunch

6 Which word should have a capital letter in this sentence?

it was a mug.

- it
- was
- mug

GO ON

Name ______________________ Date ________

7 Which word is **wrong** in this sentence?

"I know what I will gives Mom this time," Lee said.

- ⬭ know
- ⬭ gives
- ⬭ time

8 Which word is **wrong** in this sentence?

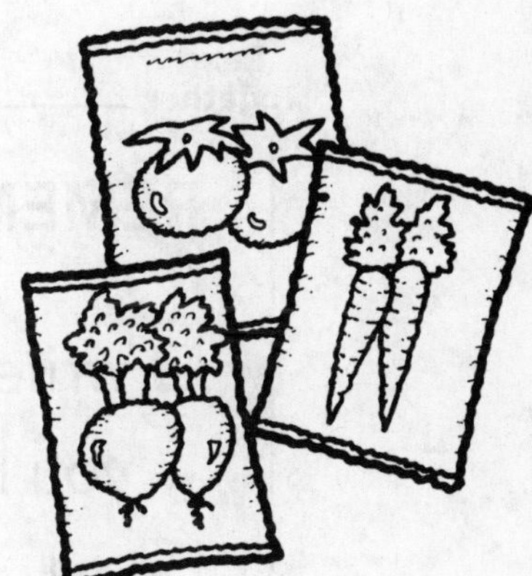

"I am go to get her some plant seeds."

- ⬭ go
- ⬭ some
- ⬭ seeds

9 Which word is spelled **wrong** in this sentence?

"Mom likes to grai plants," Lee said.

- ⬭ likes
- ⬭ grai
- ⬭ plants

10 Which punctuation mark should come at the end of this sentence?

Which seeds will Lee get __

- ⬭ .
- ⬭ ?
- ⬭ !

Name ______________________________ Date ______

Writing: Written Compositon

Read Together

Write about a problem you had, and tell how you solved it.

Read Together

REMEMBER, YOU SHOULD

- ❑ write a true story about a problem you had
- ❑ tell about your problem in the beginning, and tell how you solved it in the middle and end
- ❑ use order words, such as *first*, *next*, *then*, and *last*, when they help tell the story
- ❑ use the sounds in the words to help you write them
- ❑ begin each sentence with a capital letter

To the teacher: Read this page with children. Have them plan their story on a separate sheet. Direct them to use the following lined pages for writing their story.

Name ____________________ Date ______

BE SURE TO WRITE YOUR STORY ON THESE LINES.

Name ______________________ Date ______

Name ____________________ Date ______________

Reading

Read Together

Read the story. Then read each question with your teacher. Mark the space for the best answer to each question.

What a Kite!

The Young family went to the park. They took a lunch. While eating, Carl and Joy watched some girls and boys fly kites.

"I wish we had a kite," said Joy. "It would be fun to fly it."

"We'll come to the park again," said Joy's mother. "Then we will bring a kite."

"Wait!" said Carl. "I <u>know</u> what we can do."

To the teacher: Read the directions and questions with children. Passage and answer choices should be read independently.

Carl ran to the car. He got some yarn that was in his mother's bag. Then he got their lunch bag. Carl fixed the yarn to the open end of the bag.

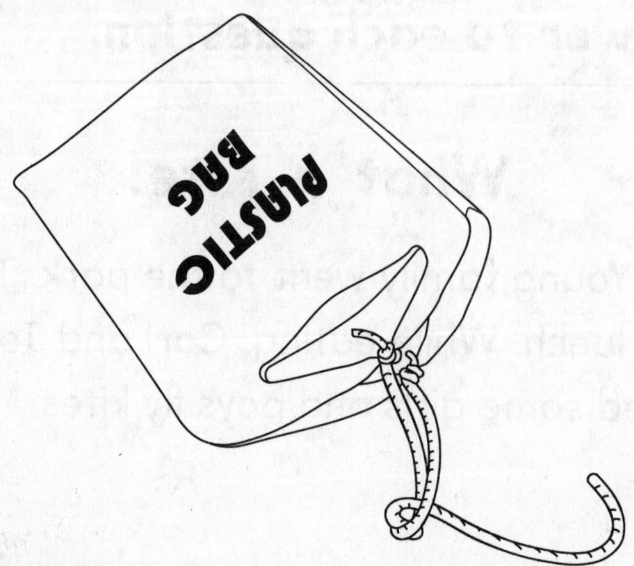

"Here, Joy," Carl said. "Run with the yarn to make the bag fly." In no time, Joy had the kite flying.

Joy said, "It may not be a real kite, but it is still fun."

And it was.

Name ______________________ Date ____________

1 What is Joy's problem in this story?

- ⬭ She wants a kite.
- ⬭ She wants to eat lunch.
- ⬭ She wants to run with Jake.

2 Read this sentence from the story.

"I <u>know</u> what we can do."

What does the underlined word mean?

- ⬭ have a plan
- ⬭ see a friend
- ⬭ like to make

3 Read this sentence from the story.

Carl ran to the <u>car</u>.

What does the underlined word mean?

- ⬭ a playground
- ⬭ a tray that holds food
- ⬭ a ride that has wheels

Name ______________________ Date ____________

4 What happens right after Carl gets some yarn?

- ⬭ The family eats lunch.
- ⬭ Carl gets the lunch bag.
- ⬭ Joy watches boys and girls fly kites.

5 Read this sentence from the story.

Carl fixed the yarn to the open end of the bag.

Which word in the sentence is an action verb?

- ⬭ fixed
- ⬭ the
- ⬭ yarn

6 What happens after Carl gives Joy the bag with the yarn?

- ⬭ Joy blows on it.
- ⬭ Joy runs with it.
- ⬭ Joy puts it in the car.

GO ON

Name ______________________ Date ______________

7 Which word tells how Joy feels at the end of the story?

- glad
- mad
- sad

8 Mother is one of the characters in the story. Which group does the word <u>mother</u> fit into?

- flowers
- family
- food

GO ON

Name ____________________ Date ____________

Read Together

Read the selection. Then read each question with your teacher. Mark the space for the best answer to each question.

Ants

Ants live in many places. They are very small. Ants live in a big family. An ant family lives in a nest. Ant nests can be in the ground or on <u>top</u> of the ground. <u>Some</u> ants make nests in trees.

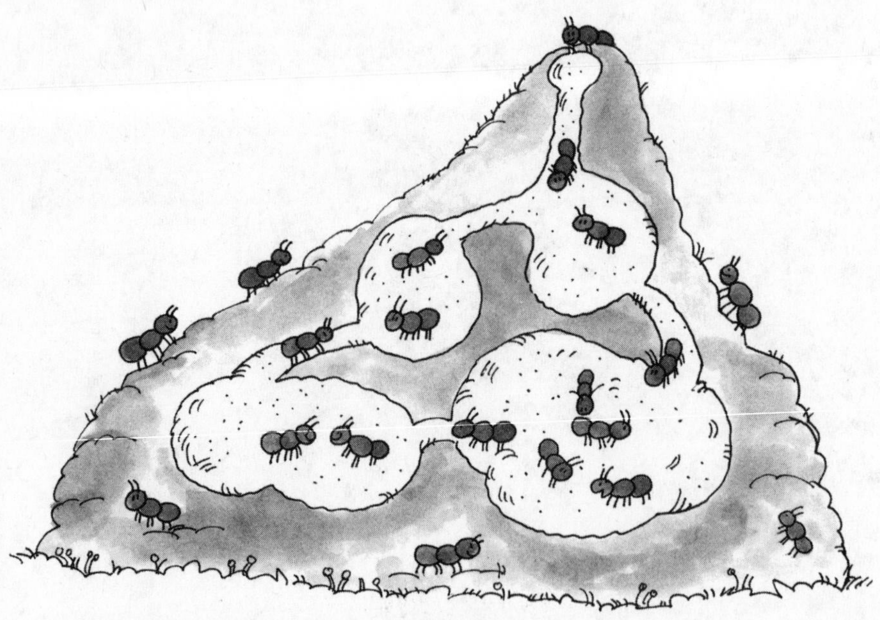

To the teacher: Read the directions and questions with children. Passage and answer choices should be read independently.

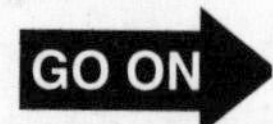

Name ______________________ Date ____________

Ants have jobs to do. Each ant does one job, but the ants work together like a team. One ant is the queen. Just one queen lives in a nest. The queen lays eggs. That is her main job.

Some ants clean the nest. Some ants look for food, like seeds. They bring the food back to the nest. One group of ants feeds <u>baby</u> ants. All the ants work hard. It helps the family grow.

GO ON

Name ______________________ Date ____________

9 What does the title tell you about the selection?

- It will tell about ants.
- It will tell about queens.
- It will tell about a family.

10 Read this sentence from the selection.

Ant nests can be in the ground or on top of the ground.

What does top mean in this sentence?

- a shirt
- a toy that spins
- the part that is up

11 Read this sentence from the selection.

Some ants make nests in trees.

What does the underlined word mean?

- all
- just one
- not many

GO ON

12 What is the main job of the queen?

- ⬭ to lay eggs
- ⬭ to look for food
- ⬭ to clean the nest

13 Read this sentence from the selection.

One group of ants feeds <u>baby</u> ants.

What does the underlined word mean?

- ⬭ an old animal
- ⬭ animals that work
- ⬭ a very young animal

14 Which sentence tells the main idea of "Ants"?

- ⬭ An ant family lives in a nest.
- ⬭ Ants have jobs that help their family.
- ⬭ Some ants look for food to bring to the nest.

15 Why did the author write "Ants"?

- ⬭ to tell a funny tale
- ⬭ to tell facts about ants
- ⬭ to get kids to work hard like ants

Name ______________________ Date ____________

Reading: Phonics

Read Together

Read each sentence. Then mark the space for the word that best completes the sentence.

16 Can a rock be a funny pet?
Follow these ________ to make
a pet rock.

- ⬭ steps
- ⬭ stops
- ⬭ steep

17 First, you will ________ to find
a rock.

- ⬭ nail
- ⬭ need
- ⬭ nod

18 Look for one ________ is small
and round.

- ⬭ chat
- ⬭ hat
- ⬭ that

To the teacher: Read the directions with children. Items and answer choices should be read independently.

GO ON

Name ____________________ Date __________

19 The rock should be ______, too.

- smell
- smooth
- smith

20 Next, wash the ______ off.

- sail
- seal
- soil

21 Then, pick a ______ or zoo animal to make.

- farm
- firm
- foam

22 Now ______ the parts on the animal.

- paint
- pant
- point

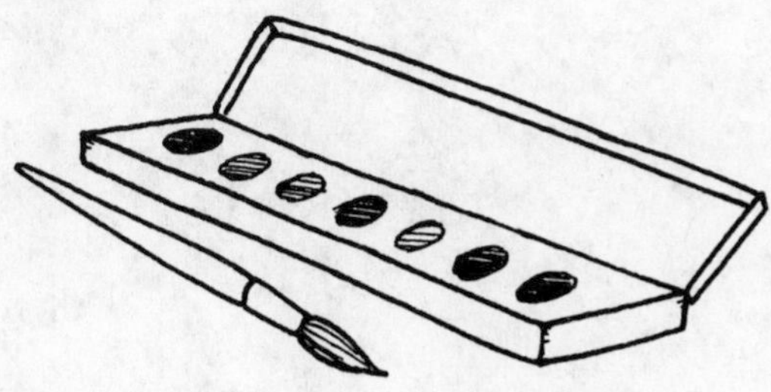

Name ____________________ Date ____________

23 You can add things like the ______, paws, and tail.

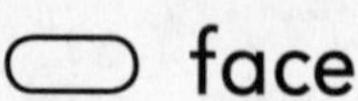 face
⬭ fuss
⬭ fast

24 Set the rock on paper until the paint ______ wet.

 I'm
⬭ isn't
⬭ it's

25 It will not be ______ before you have a pet rock!

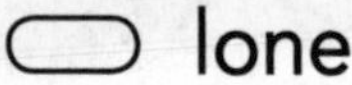 lone
⬭ long
⬭ lost

Name ____________________ Date ____________

Writing: Revising and Editing

Read Together

Read each question with your teacher. Decide which is the best answer. Then mark the space for answer you have chosen.

1 Which word should go in the blank in this sentence?

Next week, my family ______ sell some things.

- ⬭ will
- ⬭ had
- ⬭ was

2 Which words should go in the blank in this sentence?

______ looked for things to sell.

- ⬭ Mom and I
- ⬭ I and Mom
- ⬭ Mom and me

To the teacher: Read the directions and questions with children. Target sentences and answer choices should be read independently.

Name ______________________ Date __________

3 Which word in this sentence is spelled **wrong**?

My dod helped, too.

- dod
- helped
- too

4 Which punctuation mark should come at the end of this sentence?

Do you know what we found

- .
- ?
- !

5 Which word tells about the dishes in this sentence?

Mom pulled out some blue dishes.

- pulled
- out
- blue

GO ON

Name ______________________ Date ____________

6 Which word should go in the blank in this sentence?

The dishes ________ a gift.

- ⬭ was
- ⬭ were
- ⬭ is

7 Which word should go in the blank in this sentence?

One of ________ friends gave the dishes to us.

- ⬭ her
- ⬭ hers
- ⬭ she

8 Which word is **wrong** in this sentence?

Then we looked at all of my toy.

- ⬭ looked
- ⬭ my
- ⬭ toy

GO ON

Name ________________________ Date ______________

9 Which word should go in the blank in this sentence?

I am ______ to sell the ones I don't like.

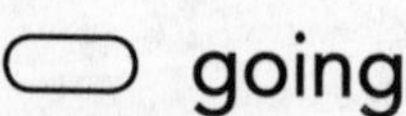

- ⬭ going
- ⬭ go
- ⬭ will

10 Which word in this sentence is spelled **wrong**?

Now my toy box will nat be so full.

- ⬭ will
- ⬭ nat
- ⬭ so

STOP

Name ______________________ Date ____________

Writing: Written Composition

Read Together

Write a make-believe story about an animal that looks for a new home.

Read Together

REMEMBER, YOU SHOULD

- ❑ write about an animal that looks for a new home
- ❑ make sure your story has a beginning, a middle, and an ending
- ❑ use the sounds in the words to help you write them
- ❑ write sentences that have different lengths

To the teacher: Read this page with children. Have them plan their story on a separate sheet of paper. Direct them to use the following lined pages for writing their story.

Name ____________________ Date ____________

BE SURE TO WRITE YOUR STORY ON THESE LINES.

Name ______________________ Date ____________

Reading

Read Together

Read the story. Then read each question with your teacher. Mark the space for the best answer to each question.

The Boat Ride

Fred Frog lived in a pond. He loved to swim in the cold water.

One day Bud Bird came to see Fred.

"Hello, Bud!" Fred called out. "It is a nice day!"

"Yes, it is," said Bud. "But it is a little hot. I wish I could swim like you. Swimming is too hard to do."

Fred didn't want Bud to be unhappy. He had an idea!

To the teacher: Read the directions and questions with children. Passages and answer choices should be read independently.

Fred swam to some leaves. He got the biggest one. He quickly pushed it near Bud. Bud hopped on. The leaf was a boat.

"This is not too hard to do. This is a breeze!" cried Bud. "I am not hot now! Thank you, Fred!"

Name ______________________ Date ______

1 Where does the story take place?

- at a park
- at a pond
- at a school

2 When does the story take place?

- on a cold day
- on a rainy day
- on a sunny day

3 Read this sentence from the story.

He loved to swim in the cold water.

What does the underlined word mean in this sentence?

- did not like
- liked a lot
- liked a little

GO ON

Name ______________________ Date ________

4 How is Fred different from Bud?

- ⬭ Fred can fly.
- ⬭ Fred can swim.
- ⬭ Fred eats bugs.

5 Read this sentence from the story.

Fred didn't want Bud to be unhappy.

Which group does the word unhappy fit into?

- ⬭ feelings
- ⬭ family
- ⬭ time

6 Read this sentence from the story.

He quickly pushed it near Bud.

What does the underlined word mean in this sentence?

- ⬭ out of
- ⬭ close to
- ⬭ far away

GO ON

7 Read these sentences from the story.

> "This is not too hard to do. <u>This is a breeze</u>!" cried Bud.

What does <u>this is a breeze</u> mean in this sentence?

- ⬭ It is easy.
- ⬭ It is windy.
- ⬭ It feels cold.

8 Use the chart to answer the question below.

How Bud Feels	
At Beginning of Story	At End of Story
upset, hot	

Which words go in the empty box to tell how Bud feels at the end?

- ⬭ sad, cool
- ⬭ mad, hot
- ⬭ glad, cool

GO ON

Name ____________________ Date ________

Read Together

Read the selection. Then read each question with your teacher. Mark the space for the best answer to each question.

A Sailboat Needs Wind

You can ride in a sailboat. It will take you across the water. A sailboat is unlike most boats. It does not use gas to make it go. It uses wind!

A sailboat has a large sail. It is made of cloth. People lift the sail high on a pole.

To the teacher: Read the directions and questions with children. Passages and answer choices should be read independently.

Name ______________________ Date ______

Wind pushes things. For sailing, it should be blowing behind the boat. Wind fills the sail. The cloth blocks the wind. The wind keeps pushing on the sail. It makes the boat go.

A strong wind makes the boat go faster. If the wind stops, the boat will stop, too.

9 What does the title tell you the selection will be about?

- ⬭ a kite
- ⬭ a sailboat
- ⬭ a family at a lake

10 Read this sentence from the selection.

You can <u>ride</u> in a sailboat.

What does the word <u>ride</u> mean in this sentence?

- ⬭ get in and go
- ⬭ something at a park
- ⬭ to throw something away

11 Read this sentence from the selection.

A sailboat is <u>unlike</u> most boats.

What does the word <u>unlike</u> mean in this sentence?

- ⬭ not like
- ⬭ just like
- ⬭ like again

GO ON

Name ______________________ Date ______

12 Why does the wind push a sailboat?

- People lift it up.
- The sail blocks it.
- It makes the pole bend into the water.

13 Read this sentence from the selection.

A sailboat has a <u>large</u> sail.

What does the underlined word mean in this sentence?

- big
- many
- white

14 How do the pictures help you know more about a sail?

- They show how people lift it.
- They show what it looks like.
- They show how people make it.

15 What does a strong wind do to a sailboat?

- It makes the sailboat stop.
- It makes the sailboat go faster.
- It makes the sailboat slow down.

STOP

Name ______________________________ Date ______

Reading: Phonics

Read Together

Read the sentences. Then mark the space for the word that best completes each sentence.

16 The sun's ________ woke Jean.

- list
- late
- light

17 She ________ out of bed.

- hoped
- hopped
- hot

18 She got dressed ________.

- quiz
- quite
- quickly

To the teacher: Read the directions with children. Items and answer choices should be read independently.

Name ______________________ Date ______

19 Jean was feeling ______.

- ⬭ happy
- ⬭ happen
- ⬭ hay

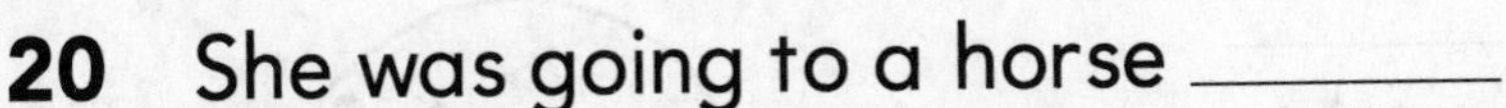

20 She was going to a horse ______.

- ⬭ stacking
- ⬭ stable
- ⬭ stamps

21 She was not going to be ______.

- ⬭ she
- ⬭ shine
- ⬭ shy

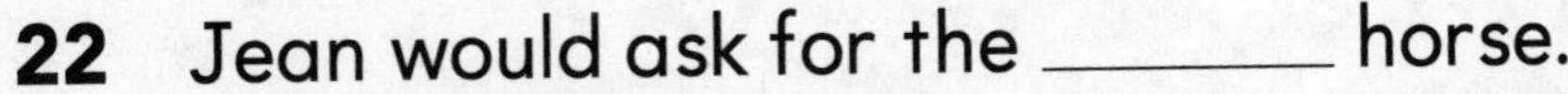

22 Jean would ask for the ______ horse.

- ⬭ nicest
- ⬭ nicyest
- ⬭ niciest

GO ON

23 She did not want to be ______.

- ⬭ unsay
- ⬭ unsafe
- ⬭ untie

24 She packed a helmet ______ she could put it on her head.

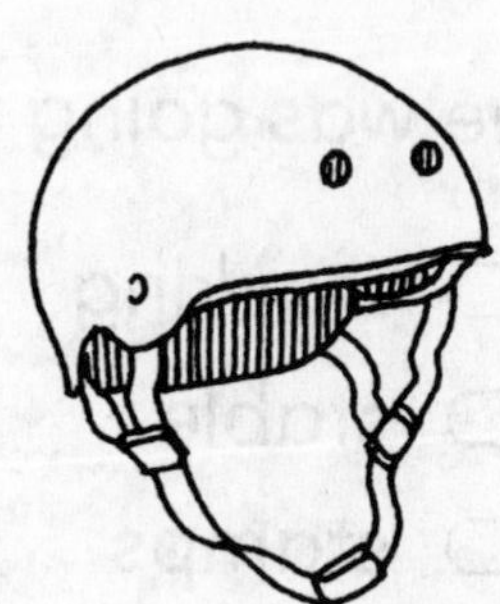

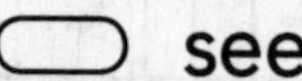

- ⬭ see
- ⬭ say
- ⬭ so

25 It was in her ______ backpack.

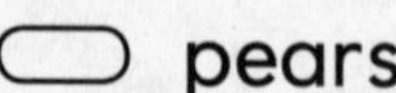

- ⬭ pears
- ⬭ purple
- ⬭ pull

STOP

Name ______________________ Date ________

Writing: Revising and Editing

Read Together

Read each question with your teacher. Decide which is the best answer. Then mark the space for the answer you have chosen.

1 Which word is spelled **wrong** in this sentence?

Gail wanted to make a pai.

- ⬭ wanted
- ⬭ make
- ⬭ pai

2 Which word is spelled **wrong** in this sentence?

She looked at the peaches on the tawble.

- ⬭ looked
- ⬭ peaches
- ⬭ tawble

To the teacher: Read the directions and questions with children. Target sentences and answer choices should be read independently.

Name ______________________ Date ______

3 Which word should go in the blank in this sentence?

The fuzzy peaches had a ________ smell.

- ⬭ sweet
- ⬭ bumpy
- ⬭ loud

4 Which punctuation mark should come at the end of this sentence?

Could Gail use them to bake a good treat

- ⬭ .
- ⬭ ?
- ⬭ !

5 Which word should go in the blank in this sentence?

Gail picked up the ________ peach of all.

- ⬭ big
- ⬭ bigger
- ⬭ biggest

GO ON

6 Which word in this sentence tells how the peach felt to Gail?

The peach was too hard.

⬭ was
⬭ too
⬭ hard

7 Which word should go in the blank in this sentence?

"Come try the plums over ______," said Ron.

⬭ here
⬭ this
⬭ when

8 Which punctuation mark should come at the end of this sentence?

Gail took a bite of a plum

⬭ .
⬭ ?
⬭ ,

9 Which word should go in the blank in this sentence?

The plum was ______ good.

- ⬭ soft
- ⬭ very
- ⬭ walk

10 Which punctuation mark should come at the end of this sentence?

These plums are yummy

- ⬭ ,
- ⬭ ?
- ⬭ !

Name ____________________ Date ______

Writing: Written Compositon

Read Together

Write a paragraph to tell why you like your favorite story.

Read Together

REMEMBER, YOU SHOULD

- ❏ write a topic sentence that tells what your favorite story is
- ❏ write detail sentences that tell what you like about that story
- ❏ indent the first sentence of the paragraph
- ❏ use the sounds in the words to help you write them

To the teacher: Read this page with children. Have them plan their paragraph on a separate sheet. Direct them to the following lined pages for writing.

Name ____________________ Date ________

Grade 1, Unit 6
UNIT TEST

Written Composition

BE SURE TO WRITE YOUR PARAGRAPH ON THESE LINES.

Name ______________________ Date ______

Grade 1, Unit 6
UNIT TEST

Written Composition

JOURNEYS

Benchmark and Unit Tests

Grade 1

ISBN-13: 978-0-547-36884-9
ISBN-10: 0-547-36884-4

HOUGHTON MIFFLIN HARCOURT
School Publishers